Copyright © 2017 Ann M Hawkins
All rights reserved.

ISBN 13: 978-1545365656
ISBN 10: 1545365652

Wrapped in the protection of a soft green leaf on a strong twisted branch, a little acorn drifted off to sleep. "Sleep Cornelia," Mother Oak whispered in the gentle rustling of her leaves as a warm summer breeze whirled through her branches.

"I will tell you a story about when I was a small tree growing up in the shadow of the oldest oak tree in the forest. It was more than a hundred years ago, and the forest was full of life."

"Animals climbed in the trees and played on the forest floor, as they had for centuries."

"The giant oak tree provided them with food, shelter, and comfort."

"Each spring, songbirds would return to the forest and fill the air with their beautiful music."

"Butterflies would float high above me. When they came to rest on my delicate green leaves, they decorated me like ribbons in a child's hair."

"Forest creatures would share with me the adventures they'd had in the meadow and near the river where they drank the cold, clear water as it foamed and hurried by them."

"The old oak tree promised me that someday I, too, would be tall enough to see the wonders that lay beyond the thickness of the woods."

Inspired by Alex Saberi photography

"One spring evening, a storm howled through the forest. The starless night shook with thunder as each brilliant flash of lightning raced across the sky."

"Suddenly, a lightning bolt – frighteningly beautiful – hurled itself at the old oak tree. The sound the lightning made as it struck her massive trunk could be heard for miles. A fire followed but only burned for a short while before the cool, wet rain fell heavily, easing the old tree's struggle. The old oak tree fell onto the forest floor with a thunder of her own."

Mother oak rocked Cornelia while she remembered how the old oak tree comforted her all those years ago. "The old oak tree had said, 'Do not be afraid, for this is God's way. It is time for me to lie down and make room for you and the other small trees to grow tall and strong. I have lived many years.'"

"'Each year I stood in the stillness of winter and watched snow silently cover the distant mountaintop.'"

"I waited each spring for the sun to melt the icy peaks, which sent the cold, clear water down the mountain's rugged face - tears of joy for another new beginning."

"I marveled at the many rainbows that magically appeared over the meadow after warm summer showers fell gently down from heaven.'"

Cornelia yawned and grew heavy in Mother Oak's branches. Mother Oak brushed a leaf away from Cornelia's face and continued.

"Then the old oak told me that she could still remember the feel of the crisp autumn wind blowing through a kaleidoscope of colorful branches - sending her last generation of brown, crisp leaves to dance over her roots."

"The old oak tree then wondered with pride at just how many animals she had fed and sheltered in the three hundred years she had lived upon the earth."

"She smiled lovingly as she remembered the many baby birds that had taken flight from her sprouting arms."

As the old oak tree's magnificent branches faded into the ground beneath her, she nourished the soil giving back to the earth all it had given to her. The sky where her lush canopy once rose was now filled with sunlight that filtered down to the forest floor.

As weeks turned into years…

And as years turned into decades...

"I grew tall," said Mother Oak.

"My leaves were bathed in sunlight and my roots were buried deep in rich soil."

"Soon I would be tall enough to see all of the wonderful sights the old oak had promised, and I wondered: Would the river be running fast enough for me to see it tumble past the edge of the forest? What does a rainbow look like, stretched end to end over a humming meadow?"

Inspired by Jurek Grzesiak photography

"I slept restlessly that winter long ago. I could feel the old oak tree deep within me, eager to peek above the tree line once again."

"As I felt the first drops of spring rain, I lifted my face toward the sky, and…. I began to weep."

"Many changes had taken place in the forest since the old oak tree had fallen."

"The mountain could be seen in the distance, but no trees grew upon its side. The river no longer cascaded down its face to flow to the edge of the forest, and the meadow was gone too, for it had no river to feed it. Now, the forest stops a short distance from where we live and grow."

Cornelia slumbered. Soon she would fall and grow roots in the earth beneath her. Sadly, Mother oak wondered: What stories about the forest will Cornelia have to whisper to her sleeping acorns?

What stories about the forest will you have to whisper to yours?

RECYCLE
COMPOST
LEARN
CONSERVE
PROTECT

GET INVOLVED

Children can HELP the World's forests, rivers, meadows, and oceans!

Thank you to my family and friends for your support and encouragement over the 18 years it took me to complete this labor of love.

A special thank you to my cousin Rick for putting the color back into my illustrations.

To Royale – you shared your love of a well-worn children's book with me and helped to edit my story without changing the way I intended it to be. I can't thank you enough for that.

Finally, to my son, Jeremy – I am grateful for everything you did to make my dream a reality. Your patience, support, and technical help got me over the finish line!

Made in the USA
Monee, IL
08 January 2023

24850540R00038